The

Great Massachusetts

Puzzle Book

by Jane Petrlik Smolik

MidRun Press
Wenham, Massachusetts 01984

For
"The Cousins"

Special thanks to my children, Libby, Taylor, Adrienne and Chris Smolik and to their cousins Sam and Emily Hutchinson, Holly, Katie and Will Yermal for their enthusiasm. And now we celebrate the "little cousins", Jack and Ronan Cardus and Mary Jane Petrlik.♡

ISBN-13: 978-0-9664095-5-0
ISBN-10: 0-9664095-5-8

Table of Contents

The Salem Witch Museum

The little witch has lost her way. Help her find the path back to The Salem Witch Museum.

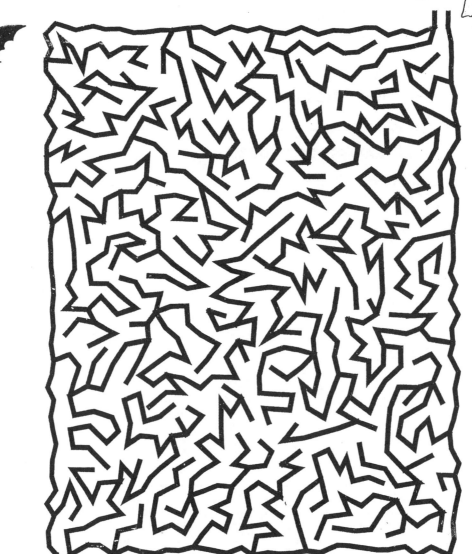

What kind of witch lives at the beach? A sand-witch.

 # Sea Glass

Along our beaches people love to collect small pieces of sparkling, jewel-like sea glass. These bits of beach glass start out as shards of glass or pottery from ship wrecks, pirates and even littering. They become smooth after being rolled about by the abrasive sand. They are so beautiful that jewelers make bracelets and necklaces from them and people collect them as souvenirs. The ruby red pieces are the rarest!

It is not just bottles that become precious sea glass though. Fill in the Kriss-Kross with 16 items that can end up as sparkling sea glass treasure.

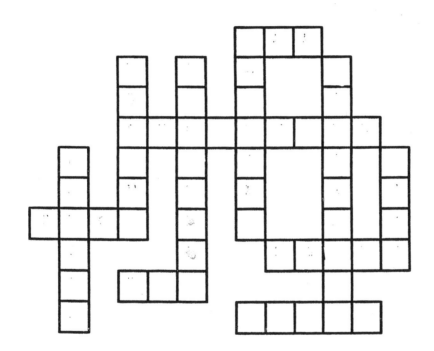

3 Letters	5 Letters	7 Letters	9 Letters
JAR	CHINA	JEWELRY	PORCELAIN
TOY	PLATE		STONEWARE

4 Letters	6 Letters	8 Letters
JUGS	DISHES	CROCKERY
PIPE	SAUCER	

Five Senses in Massachusetts

There are many things to see, hear, taste and smell in the great state of Massachusetts. Put a check mark in the box next to each thing you have experienced.

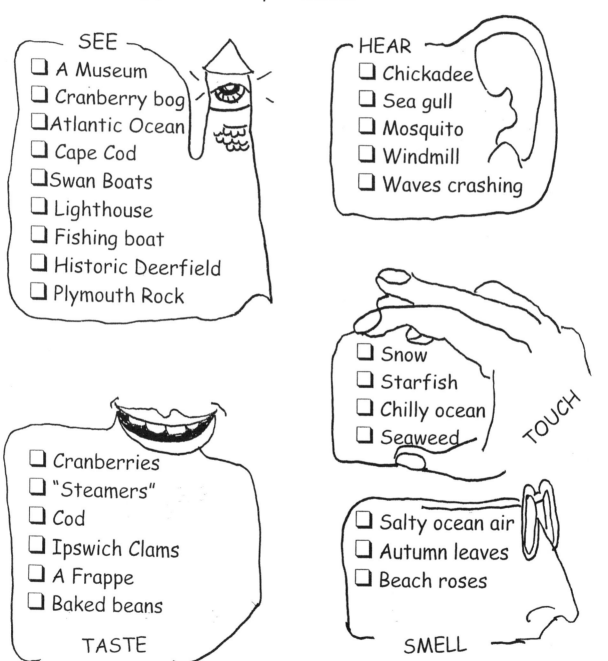

SEE
- ❑ A Museum
- ❑ Cranberry bog
- ❑ Atlantic Ocean
- ❑ Cape Cod
- ❑ Swan Boats
- ❑ Lighthouse
- ❑ Fishing boat
- ❑ Historic Deerfield
- ❑ Plymouth Rock

HEAR
- ❑ Chickadee
- ❑ Sea gull
- ❑ Mosquito
- ❑ Windmill
- ❑ Waves crashing

TOUCH
- ❑ Snow
- ❑ Starfish
- ❑ Chilly ocean
- ❑ Seaweed

TASTE
- ❑ Cranberries
- ❑ "Steamers"
- ❑ Cod
- ❑ Ipswich Clams
- ❑ A Frappe
- ❑ Baked beans

SMELL
- ❑ Salty ocean air
- ❑ Autumn leaves
- ❑ Beach roses

Arnold Arboretum Maze

An arboretum is a place where they collect woody plants (trees). The Arnold Arboretum in Jamaica Plain has more than 13,000 trees, shrubs, and other plants. On Mother's Day, families love to come here to enjoy the beautiful smelling lilacs. Jacob has gotten separated from his family and lost among all the trees. Help him find his way back to his family.

Criss-Cross Capes

Along the coastline of Massachusetts there are many *capes*. A *cape* is a pointed piece of land that extends into the sea beyond the rest of the shoreline.

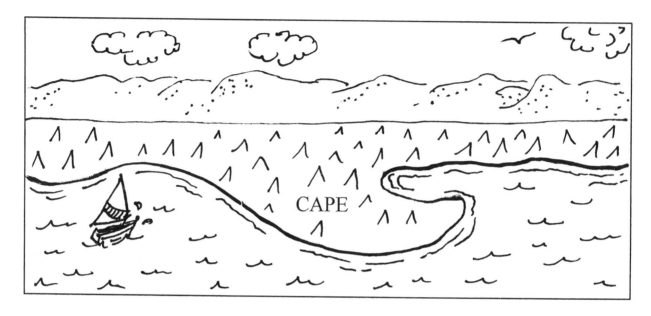

Six of these capes have been named. Using the word box below, fit the names into the criss-cross grid. We've filled in the letter "E" to get you started.

WORD BOX

7 Letters
CAPE ANN
CAPE COD

8 Letters
CAPE POGE
CAPE POND

9 Letters
CAPE HEDGE

11 Letters
CAPE HIGGINS

The Old Ball Game

Massachusetts has some of the greatest fans to cheer on some of the greatest sports teams in the country.

Beside each sport, put the letter of the team that plays that game.

B. Red Sox   **E. Patriots**   **A. Celtics**

D. Bruins   **C. Revolution**

1. ____ Baseball

2. ____ Football

3. ____ Basketball

4. ____ Hockey

5. ____ Soccer

11

Now match the team with its home location. Hint: some teams play in the same location as other teams.

A. Gillette Stadium   **B. Fenway Park**   **C. TD Banknorth Garden**

1. ____ Red Sox

2. ____ Patriots

3. ____ Celtics

4. ____ Bruins

5. ____ Revolution

SEARCHING FOR SEUSS

Question: In what Massachusetts city was Theodore Geisel (better known as Dr. Seuss) born?

Find the one letter in the word in the left-hand column that is not in the word in the right-hand column. Write the extra letter in the blank space. Then read down the column for the answer.

SEAT ___	TEA
SPRING ___	RINGS
TIRE ___	TIE
HIDES ___	SHED
WINTER ___	WRITE
GHOST ___	SHOT
FEAT ___	ATE
IRATE ___	TEAR
BEAST ___	STAB
LEAST ___	SEAT
DREAM ___	MARE

12

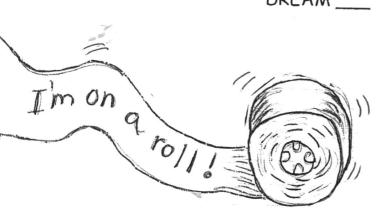

Librarian: Knock-knock.
Student: Who's there?
Librarian: Winnie.
Student: Winnie who?
Librarian: Winnie you going to bring back those overdue books?

Knock-knock.
Who's there?
Rita.
Rita who?
Rita lot of good books!

The Dot Game

This game needs two players. Take turns drawing a horizontal or vertical line between two dots. The player that draws a line that completes a square writes his or her initial inside that completed square. It helps if you each use a different colored pencil or pen. When all the squares are connected, count how many squares each player finished. Squares are worth one point each or two points if it contains a chickadee. Whoever has the most points wins.

The chickadee is the Official State Bird. They got their name because when they call it sounds like: "chick-adee-dee-dee".

True or False

Question: What is the official state insect of Massachusetts?

Some of the sentences below are true and others are false. If the statement is true, enter the letter from the True column on the empty space next to that sentence. If it is false, write the letter from the False column in the blank space next to that sentence. When you're finished, read down the right hand Answer column to find the official state insect.

	TRUE	FALSE	BLANK
1. Martha's Vineyard is an island off the coast of Massachusetts.	L	B	_____
2. Worcester is the capital of Massachusetts.	F	A	_____
3. The Connecticut River flows into Boston Harbor.	E	D	_____
4. Salem is well known for the witch trials that took place there.	Y	S	_____
5. Beacon Hill is a neighborhood located in the city of Lowell.	T	B	_____
6. Mt. Greylock is the highest spot in Massachusetts.	U	K	_____
7. The swan boats are a famous ride in Boston's Public Garden.	G	L	_____

GOOD NEIGHBORS!

Massachusetts shares borders with 5 other states. Read the directions below and then label that state on the map.

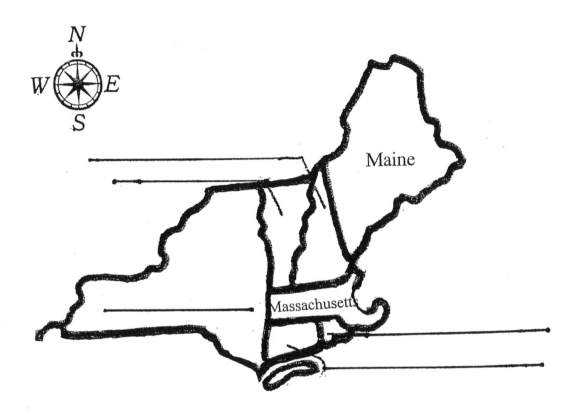

      1. <u>New Hampshire</u> is north of Massachusetts and also shares a border with Maine.

      2. <u>Vermont</u> is north of Massachusetts and shares its western border with New York.

      3. <u>New York</u> is west of Massachusetts and is the largest state bordering Massachusetts.

      4. <u>Rhode Island</u> lies south of Massachusetts and is the smallest state to share a border with us.

      5. <u>Connecticut</u> lies south of Massachusetts and also shares borders with New York and Rhode Island.

Famous From Massachusetts

    Theodor Geisel was born in Springfield, Massachusetts in 1904 but you probably know him by the name he used later in his life - Dr. Seuss. Seuss was his mother's maiden name and his middle name.

    Early in his life, he'd planned on becoming a professor. But when he found himself sitting in class doodling much of the time, he wisely decided to become an artist instead.

    While sailing on a luxury ship, Seuss was inspired by the rhythm of its engines and he used that sound as the inspiration for his first children's book *And to Think I Saw It On Mulberry Street.* He received 27 rejections from 27 publishers before one finally accepted it. Remember that the next time you feel like giving up!

    Until then children's books were often dull and boring. A friend of Seuss' bet him $50 that he couldn't write a fun book using only 50 words. Seuss wrote *Green Eggs and Ham.*

    Theodor Seuss Geisel died in 1991 but he continues to be the world's best-selling author of children's books.

Here are just a few of the 44 books that Dr. Seuss wrote. Put a check next to the ones you remember reading.

❑ One Fish Two Fish Red Fish Blue Fish
❑ Happy Birthday to You!
❑ The Sneetches and Other Stories
❑ All Aboard the Circus McGurkus!
❑ Oh, the Places You'll Go!
❑ Hop on Pop
❑ And to Think That I Saw In On Mulberry Street
❑ How the Grinch Stole Christmas
❑ The 500 Hats of Bartholomew Cubbins
❑ The Cat in the Hat
❑ The Butter Battle Book
❑ Green Eggs and Ham

FAMOUS FROM MASSACHUSETTS CROSSWORD
"Dr. Seuss"

After reading the brief biography of Dr. Seuss on the opposite page, see if you can do the crossword.

ACROSS

1. The rhythm of _____ inspired Seuss
5. A friend ____ Seuss $50
6. *And To Think That I Saw It On* ____ *Street*
7. Instead of teaching, Seuss became an _____
8. Children's books had become dull and _____
9. Early in life Seuss planned on being a _____
10. His first book received 27 _____
11. His full name: _____ Seuss Geisel

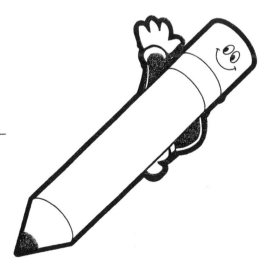

DOWN

2. Seuss' city of birth
3. Seuss' last name
4. He's still the ____ best selling author
6. "Seuss" was his mother's _____ name.

Mitten Match

After skiing, sledding and skating a pile of unmatched mittens need to be sorted. There is one mitten without a match. (This comes as no surprise to mothers.) Circle the mitten below that does not have a partner.

18

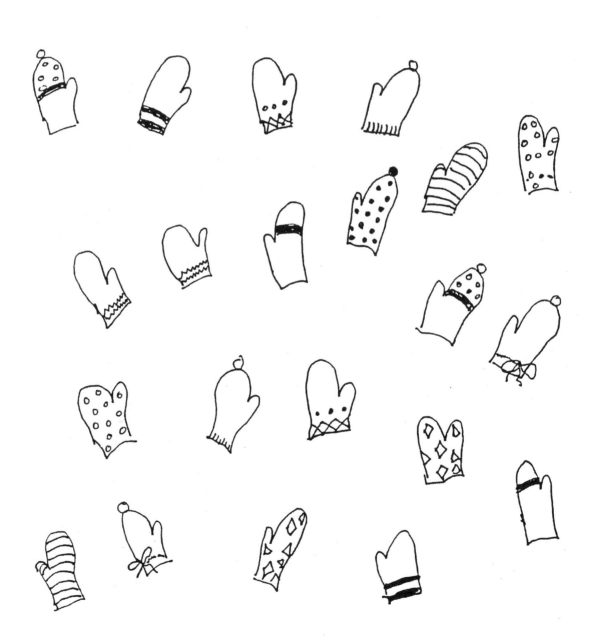

Boston Harbor Islands Criss Cross

Boston Harbor Islands is a national park area that includes 34 islands situated within the Greater Boston shoreline. Thirteen of these islands are open to visitors. Fit the thirteen islands of Boston Harbor in the Criss Cross below.

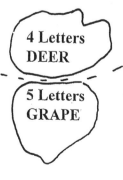

4 Letters
DEER

5 Letters
GRAPE

7 Letters
BUMPKIN
GALLOPS
GEORGES
LOVELLS

8 Letters
PEDDOCKS
THOMPSON

9 Letters
SPECTACLE
WORLDS END

13 Letters
GREAT BREWSTER
WEBB STATE PARK

14 Letters
LITTLE BREWSTER

How Many Miles?

One summer the Johnston family decided to visit some of the exciting, historic places in Massachusetts. Read each leg of the trip and then find the corresponding locations on the map on the opposite page. Write down the number of miles the family drove to get from one spot to the next. Finally, add up the miles and find out how far the family traveled that summer.

1. The Johnston family first drove from their home in Boston to the city of Lowell to learn about the Industrial Revolution at the Tsongas Industrial History Center. They drove _____ miles.

2. From Lowell they traveled west to historic Deerfield to visit this living museum. They drove _____ miles.

3. From Deerfield the family headed to Cheshire where they climbed Mt. Greylock, the highest point in Massachusetts. They drove _____ miles.

4. From Cheshire they headed east to Concord to visit the Old North Bridge. They wanted to see for themselves where "the shot heard round the world" was fired and the American Revolution began. They drove _____ miles.

5. Leaving Concord the family headed south to New Bedford overlooking Buzzards Bay. They spent the day visiting the Whaling Museum. They drove _____ miles.

6. The Johnstons left New Bedford and drove northeast to Plymouth to view Plymouth Rock where the Pilgrims first set foot on the new land. They drove _____ miles.

7. Finally, our weary travelers drove from Plymouth back home to Boston. They drove _____ miles.

Question: How many miles did the Johnston family travel that summer?
Answer: _____ miles

How Many Miles ?

Use this map to answer the questions on the opposite page.

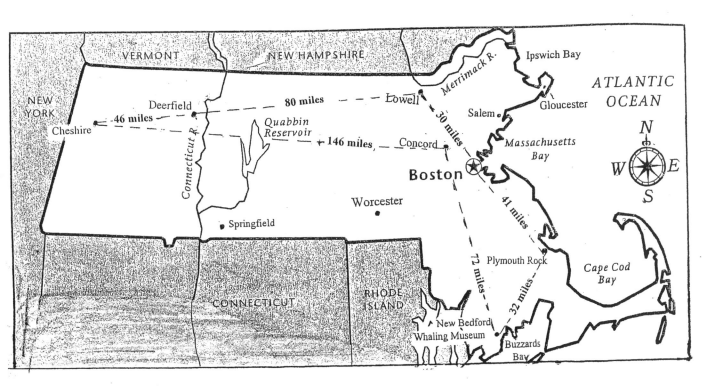

JUST RIDDLIN' AROUND

Q. What holds water but is full of holes?
A. A sponge

Q. What gets wet when drying?
A. A towel

Q. The more you take, the more you leave behind. What are they?
A. Footsteps

MUMMY IN A MAZE

The Museum of Fine Arts in Boston has some of the most important collections of art in the world. Their Egyptian Collection has statues, mummies and masks.

Help Megan find her way to the mummy through the maze below.

SEARCH FOR HISTORY

Unlike many revolutions, the Industrial Revolution did not involve guns and fighting. It was a revolution of the way people lived and worked. Instead of things being made by hand, many items began to be made in factories with large machines. People left farms and their rural homes to go to the cities and work in these factories.

This revolution of how we worked and how we made goods changed the way we lived. Thousands of people a year visit the Industrial History Center in Massachusetts with its hands-on activities.

Question: Where is this popular historical attraction located?

Find the one letter in the word in the left-hand column that is not in the word in the right hand column. Write the extra letter in the blank space. Then read down the column for the answer.

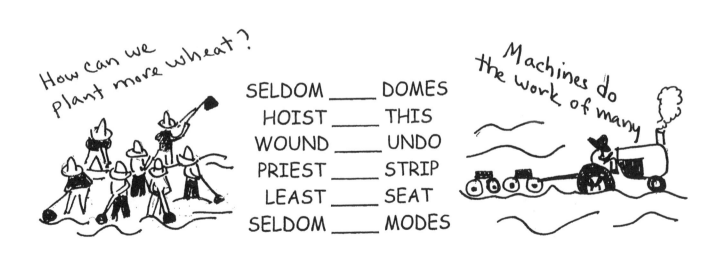

SELDOM	____	DOMES
HOIST	____	THIS
WOUND	____	UNDO
PRIEST	____	STRIP
LEAST	____	SEAT
SELDOM	____	MODES

How can we plant more wheat?

Machines do the work of many

The Quabbin Reservoir

    In the late 1890s, as the population of Boston kept increasing, the state became concerned that the existing supply of fresh, drinkable water could not keep up with the growing demand. State planners looked west to the Swift River Valley with its plentiful supply of fresh water fed by the Swift and the Ware Rivers.

    Finally, in 1927, they decided to build a huge reservoir with underground pipes that would carry water from the reservoir to the residents of Greater Boston. The only problem was that there were four towns located on the land where this huge reservoir of water would be built. The state bought up all the farms, homes and businesses in the four towns. They dug up cemeteries to move the graves. And then they demolished every building in all four towns and dug the huge hole that was to be the Quabbin Reservoir. The reservoir was 18 miles long and is one of the largest man-made public water supplies in the United States. There are lakes that aren't as big!

    While four towns were completely wiped out to build the Quabbin Reservoir, today it supplies fresh drinking water to about 2.2 million people in the Greater Boston area.

24

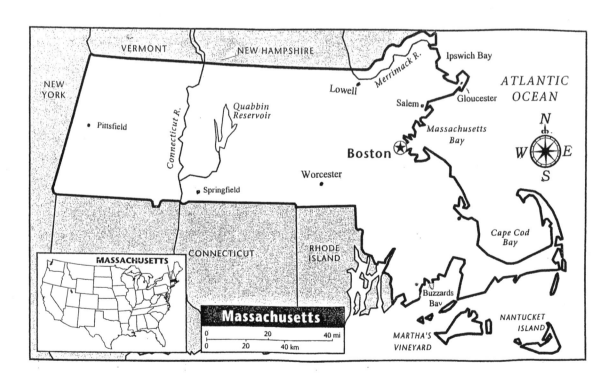

Quabbin Reservoir Word Search

While trout, salmon, bass, perch and pickerel can all be found in the waters of the Quabbin Reservoir, many animals roam in the surrounding woods and fields. Find and circle the animals listed below that live in this area.

L	E	T	M	W	M	U	S	S	O	P	P	O
P	E	N	A	E	X	Y	K	R	E	T	T	O
X	M	M	I	C	B	A	T	I	P	A	M	K
J	I	F	M	P	B	V	G	Z	S	F	C	D
S	N	O	E	I	U	O	E	L	H	U	F	U
T	K	X	C	D	N	C	B	R	H	Q	O	C
I	S	K	J	A	F	G	R	C	M	O	I	S
B	S	H	Y	I	E	R	D	O	U	I	N	I
B	Z	V	S	T	E	O	Q	M	P	Q	N	L
A	B	H	O	V	O	T	B	H	O	R	P	E
R	E	Y	A	W	Z	K	J	P	J	O	Y	Y
R	O	E	B	E	A	R	T	W	Y	H	S	M
C	B	M	U	S	K	R	A	T	G	X	Z	E

BAT
BEAR
BEAVER
BOBCAT
COYOTE
ERMINE
FISHER
FOX
LEMMING
MINK
MOOSE
MUSKRAT
OPPOSSUM
OTTER
PORCUPINE
RABBITS
WOODCHUCK

25

Q: What do ducks eat?
A: Quackers.

Following Directions

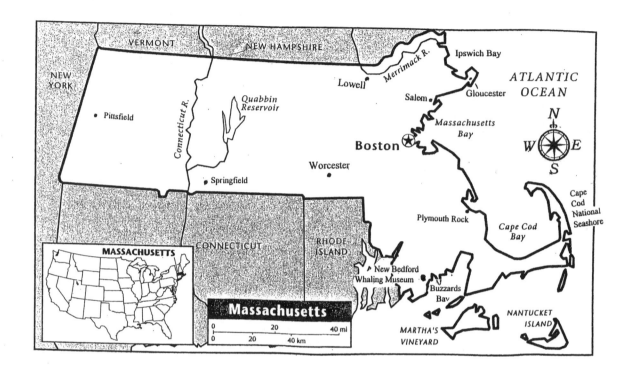

THE COMPASS ROSE

The compass rose is an icon that map makers place on a map to show which direction is north, south, east and west.

Following Directions

Using the map on the opposite page, write in what direction each location is from the other. For instance, Pittsfield is <u>NORTHWEST</u> of Springfield. The answers will be one of the following:

NORTHWEST	NORTHEAST
SOUTHWEST	SOUTHEAST

1. The Quabbin Reservoir is _____ of Worcester.

2. Pittsfield is <u>NORTHWEST</u> of Springfield.

3. Springfield is _____ of the Quabbin Reservoir.

4. Salem _____ of Boston.

5. Plymouth Rock is _____ of Boston.

6. Nantucket Island is _____ of The New Bedford Whaling Museum.

7. Buzzards Bay is _____ of Cape Cod Bay.

8. The Cape Cod National Seashore is _____ of Boston.

9. The Merrimack River is _____ of Gloucester.

10. Lowell is _____ of Boston.

11. Ipswich Bay is _____ of Boston.

27

Old Granary Burial Ground Maze

This old cemetery located behind Park Street Church holds the graves of many of Boston's most famous patriots. Paul Revere, John Hancock, Samuel Adams and the victims of the Boston Massacre have all been laid to rest at this stop along the Freedom Trail. Elizabeth Vergoose, believed to be the storyteller Mother Goose, was buried here in 1690. Help Emily find her way through the cemetery to Mother Goose's grave.

Knock, Knock!
Who's there?
Amy! Amy who?
Amy-fraid of ghosts!

SECRET MESSAGES

1. Who were the first people to inhabit Massachusetts? Cross out all the letters R, B and F to discover the answer.

RTBHEFFALGFRORNRQFUFIBARNFFINBDIBARRFNS

2. The first colonists who came to the New World were looking to have more of what? Cross out all of the letters A, C and U to discover the answer.

AUFRACEUEDCUOCMUAOUFUARAELUIGIUUON

3. A series of parks and other public green spaces that run through Boston have been given what nickname? Cross out all of the letters O, G and J to discover the answer.

JGTGJHEOJEGMEJRGALJDJOGNECGJKLACJGEOJ

4. In Boston, this walking tour guides you through the 19th-century history of the African-American community on Beacon Hill. Cross out all the letters D, S and W to discover the answer.

TDHEWSDBLWACKSWDHEWRSITWAGSEWDTRWSAISWL

Hidden Message Word Search #1

Find the words listed below and circle them. Put a cross through each one after you have found and circled it.

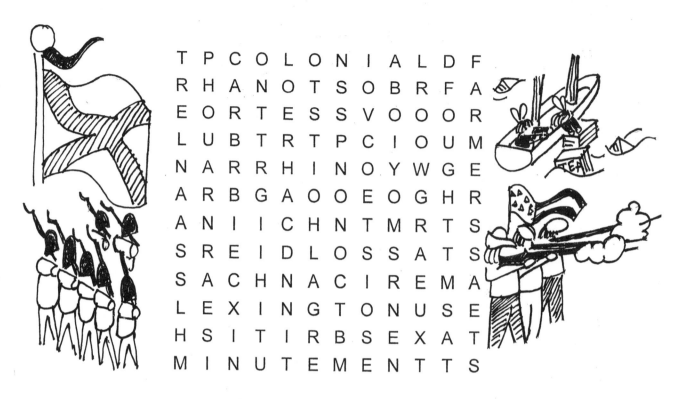

```
T P C O L O N I A L D F
R H A N O T S O B R F A
E O R T E S S V O O O R
L U B T R T P C I O U M
N A R R H I N O Y W G E
A R B G A O O E O G H R
A N I I C H N T M R T S
S R E I D L O S S A T S
S A C H N A C I R E M A
L E X I N G T O N U S E
H S I T I R B S E X A T
M I N U T E M E N T T S
```

30

AMERICAN   BOSTON   BRITISH
COLONIAL   CONCORD   FARMERS
FOUGHT   HARBOR   LEXINGTON
MINUTEMEN   PATRIOTS   RIGHTS
SOLDIERS   TAXES   TROOPS

Now fill in the spaces below with the letters that were left uncircled in the above Word Search. You will discover an interesting fact about Massachusetts.

___ _____ ____

_____ __ _____.

MISSING LETTERS

Find the one letter in the left-hand column that is not in the word in the right-hand column. Write the extra letter in the blank space. Then read down the blank column to find one of the most exciting places to visit in Massachusetts.

MEANT _____ TEAM
NOOSE _____ SOON
WILT_____ LIT

STEAM _____ MAST
PANT _____ TAP
GROUP _____ POUR
STEAL _____ SEAT
STARING _____ STRING
GRAND _____ DRAG
DREAD _____ READ

STARE _____ REST
QUEST _____ SUET
SUNDAY _____ SANDY
STATE _____ TEST
STRIDE _____ DIETS
CASHIER _____ SEARCH
UNDER _____ NERD
MINTY _____ TINY

31

Tongue Twisters

Say the following sentences as fast as you can.

Willy the whale wanders in windy, wet waves.

Beautiful Boston boasts beans, Bruins, boats and Back Bay.

Chugging down the chilly Charles chasing cheery children.

Tongue Twisters

After reading our tongue twisters, make up your own to match the pictures. We've started you.

Charming Cape Cod

_____

_____

_____

Big, bold Berkshires

_____

_____

_____

Pity the poor Pilgrims

_____

_____

_____

Algonquian Words Game

The Algonquian tribes were the first people to inhabit Massachusetts. Make as many new words as you can from the letters in "Algonquian Tribes" and write them on the lines below.

Use the scoring box to help you figure out your points for each word.

ALGONQUIAN TRIBES

WORDS	PTS.
1.	
2.	
3.	
4.	
5.	
6.	
7.	
8.	
9.	
10.	
11.	
12.	
13.	
14.	
15.	
16.	
17.	
18.	
19.	
20.	
21.	
22.	
23.	
24.	
25.	
26.	

WORDS	PTS.
27.	
28.	
29.	
30.	
31.	
32.	
33.	
34.	
35.	
36.	
37.	
38.	
39.	
40.	
41.	
42.	

YOUR SCORE _____

SCORING
3-letter word = 1 point
4-letter word = 2 points
5-letter word = 3 points
Add 1 point for each letter over 5.

Cross-Outs #1

Follow the instructions to find an interesting fact about Massachusetts.

1. Cross out 4 animals you might find in a zoo.
2. Cross out 3 colors.
3. Cross out 3 insects.
4. Cross out 1 boy's name.

MOUNT	LION	GREYLOCK	YELLOW	FLY
TIGER	IS	ZEBRA	THE	JOHN
HIGHEST	GREEN	ANT	PINK	POINT
BEE	IN	GIRAFFE	THE	STATE

Follow the instructions to find another interesting fact about Massachusetts.

1. Cross out 3 school subjects.
2. Cross out 2 fruits.
3. Cross out 3 pieces of clothing.
4. Cross out 1 fish.
5. Cross out 4 flowers.

MATH	THE	STATE'S	PANTS	NICKNAME
HISTORY	IS	PANSY	THE	PETUNIA
SHIRT	SALMON	APPLE	ENGLISH	DAFFODIL
LEMON	BAY	HAT	STATE	DAISY

Missing Letters

Question: What is the name of the mountain range that runs along the far western edge of Massachusetts?

Fill in the missing letter in the names of Massachusetts cities listed below. When all the letters are written in, read down the column for the answer.

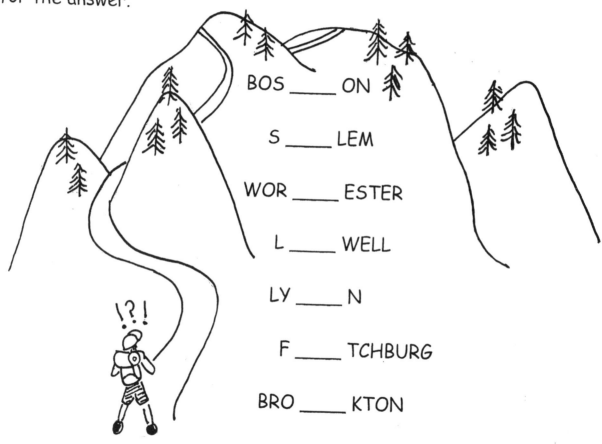

BOS ____ ON

S ____ LEM

WOR ____ ESTER

L ____ WELL

LY ____ N

F ____ TCHBURG

BRO ____ KTON

Answer: They are the _____ Mountains.

THE BOSTON MOLASSES FLOOD MAZE

On January 15, 1919 a huge vat containing 2.3 million gallons of molasses exploded with a roar. The molasses blasted through the city streets in all directions as fast as a man could run. It is believed that a sudden increase in the temperature caused the molasses to expand and the tank to explode. Help the person below flee through the streets to safety.

FAMOUS FROM MASSACHUSETTS

Many famous people were born and lived in Massachusetts. Athletes, authors, artists, inventors and politicians have all called our great state their home. Read about two of them and then solve the word search puzzle that follows. The words appear in the puzzle horizontally, vertically and diagonally.

Milton Bradley began publishing some of this country's earliest board games in Springfield in 1860. We still play Yahtzee™ and CandyLand™ today.

George S. Parker of Salem invented his first game when he was 16-years old. He and his brother, Charles, formed Parker Brothers and went on to become one of the world's largest game manufacturers. Pit™, Rook™, Risk ™ and Clue ™ are familiar to everyone. They didn't invent Monopoly™ but they produced it and it has become one of the world's most famous games.

38

BRADLEY
CANDYLAND™
CLUE™
GAMES
LOSE
MONOPOLY™
PARKER
PIT™
RISK™
ROOK™
SALEM
SPRINGFIELD
WIN
YAHTZEE™

R	S	A	N	R	E	K	R	A	P	R	D
B	I	E	D	L	V	E	A	S	O	D	L
R	P	S	M	N	M	G	O	O	L	O	W
A	I	E	K	A	A	F	K	E	S	X	I
D	T	L	O	O	G	L	I	E	Z	X	N
L	C	C	Q	J	P	F	Y	B	C	V	M
E	C	A	F	W	G	S	C	D	F	G	C
Y	J	F	Y	N	A	I	R	L	N	S	L
S	D	Y	I	L	N	Q	T	H	U	A	E
F	T	R	E	Y	B	N	J	X	R	E	C
B	P	M	Y	A	H	T	Z	E	E	L	G
S	M	O	N	O	P	O	L	Y	D	X	V

INVENT YOUR OWN GAME

It is your job to invent a new game. It can be a board game, card game or whatever you imagine would be fun. First, describe how your game would be played. Write as if you were providing the instructions to people who had never played it before.

_____
(Name of your new game)

Instructions how to play.

_____

_____

_____

_____

_____

_____

_____

_____

_____

_____

_____

The winner is the first person to _____

_____

_____

INVENT YOUR OWN GAME

Draw a sketch of what your game might look like. You can draw a board or cards or whatever you imagine!

SEAFOOD FAVORITES

The four children in the Johnson family each have a different favorite seafood they order when they go out to eat in Massachusetts. Use the information given below to find out which each child likes best. Mark an X in a square when it *cannot* be the answer. Mark an O to show the favorite seafood.

1. Clams are not Bill's favorite seafood.
2. Sue does not like cod.
3. Sarah likes quahogs better than oysters.
4. Bob's favorite are clams.
5. Sarah likes cod better than quahogs.
6. Bill prefers oyster to quahogs.

CHILD	Cod	Quahogs	Clams	Oyster
Bill				
Sarah				
Bob				
Sue				

Cape Cod Word Search

Cape Cod juts out into the Atlantic Ocean like a flexed arm. The islands of Martha's Vineyard and Nantucket lie to the south in Nantucket Sound. Thousands of people visit every year to play and swim at their sandy beaches and to enjoy the beautiful surroundings.

Find and circle 20 towns and islands that you can visit on Cape Cod.

N	W	H	M	W	O	O	D	S	H	O	L	E	I	H	Z
D	A	M	Y	A	G	F	H	T	U	O	M	L	A	F	H
B	R	N	A	A	S	D	E	N	N	I	S	T	P	C	M
A	B	A	T	H	N	H	J	V	T	P	W	T	I	A	W
R	R	Y	Y	U	T	N	P	V	X	W	E	W	H	N	E
N	E	A	W	E	C	S	I	E	I	N	R	T	W	G	L
S	W	R	A	T	N	K	A	S	E	A	A	O	Q	Y	L
T	S	M	G	Y	A	I	E	E	H	H	T	Z	Z	V	F
A	T	O	T	G	R	K	V	T	C	E	Q	E	S	M	L
B	E	U	A	Y	C	R	S	S	C	A	T	C	Y	T	E
L	R	T	F	N	L	N	E	N	A	N	K	F	H	I	E
E	J	H	A	N	A	N	I	W	N	H	T	X	M	U	T
H	L	Q	U	E	R	V	D	F	U	O	T	Y	I	T	M
L	F	O	L	U	O	D	C	X	S	Z	Z	R	Z	O	U
Q	H	R	O	R	S	Q	E	O	R	U	R	T	A	C	O
Y	O	B	P	S	A	N	D	W	I	C	H	V	C	M	F

BARNSTABLE
BOURNE
BREWSTER
CHATHAM
COTUIT
DENNIS
EASTHAM

FALMOUTH
HARWICH
HYANNIS
MARTHA'S VINEYARD
MASHPEE
NANTUCKET

ORLEANS
PROVINCETOWN
SANDWICH
TRURO
WELLFLEET
WOODS HOLE
YARMOUTH

The Pilgrims

About 400 years ago, a group of 102 English men, women and children sailed to America aboard the *Mayflower*. They left England because they wanted freedom to practice their religion as they saw fit. Most of them belonged to a religious group called the *Puritans*. They did not call themselves Pilgrims. They have been given that name because of the *pilgrimage* (or long journey) they made to the New World of America.

The Pilgrims first landed on Cape Cod but soon settled in Plymouth. According to legend, when the Pilgrims first landed in Plymouth they stepped on a granite boulder now famous as Plymouth Rock.

The first winter at Plimoth Plantation was cold and full of hardship. More than half of the Pilgrims died. Afraid that the Indians would attack them if they knew how few Pilgrims were left, they buried their dead at night with no markers on the graves.

In the spring of 1621, an Indian named Samoset walked into the village and introduced himself. Later he brought his friend Squanto to meet the settlers. Squanto taught the Pilgrims many things about surviving in this new land. He showed them how to use fish as fertilizer when planting corn, beans and pumpkins.

Eventually, with the help of Samoset and Squanto they made a peace treaty with the Wampanoag Indians who lived in the area.

They were grateful to the Indians and in the fall of 1621 they invited them to a 3-day celebration that we know as the first Thanksgiving. They played games and held jumping contests. They ate corn bread, pumpkins, carrots and onions. From the forest they cooked venison, ducks, geese, cranberries and wild turkeys. And from the waters they had eel, lobster, mussels, oyster, salmon, cod and clams. In 1863, President Abraham Lincoln proclaimed Thanksgiving a national holiday, to be celebrated the last Thursday in November. It was later changed to the fourth Thursday in November which is when we celebrate it today.

Today Plimoth (Plymouth) Plantation is the site of a living museum, dedicated to recreating the way life was for the Pilgrims. People in historic period costumes go about the daily tasks as they would have in the 17th-century. If you can't visit in person, take a virtual tour on their website www.plimoth.org/.

The Pilgrims

Use the Code Box below to write the letters above the numbered spaces and learn about the Pilgrims.

Code Box

S	J	V	D	X	I	Y	P	E	W	K	B	H
1	2	3	4	5	6	7	8	9	10	11	12	13
R	A	Q	N	G	T	L	C	M	U	Z	F	O
14	15	16	17	18	19	20	21	22	23	24	25	26

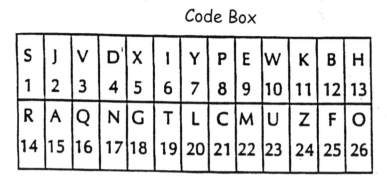

1. Indian tribe that lived in Massachusetts

__ __ __ __ __ __ __ __ __
10 15 22 8 15 17 26 15 18

2. The name of the Indian who first helped the Pilgrims

__ __ __ __ __ __ __
1   15 22 26 1 9 19

3. Name of the ship the Puritans sailed on from England.

__ __ __ __ __ __ __ __ __
22 15 7 25 20 26 10 9 14

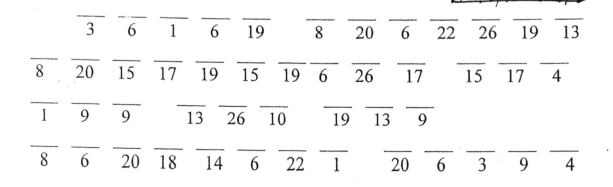

__ __ __ __ __   __ __ __ __ __ __ __
3 6 1 6 19   8 20 6 22 26 19 13

__ __ __ __ __ __ __ __ __ __   __ __ __
8 20 15 17 19 15 19 6 26 17   15 17 4

__ __ __   __ __ __   __ __ __
1 9 9   13 26 10 19 13 9

__ __ __ __ __ __ __ __   __ __ __ __ __
8 6 20 18 14 6 22 1 20 6 3 9 4

Crossword Puzzle # 1   "The Pilgrims"

Read about the Pilgrims on page 43 and then solve this puzzle. Good luck!

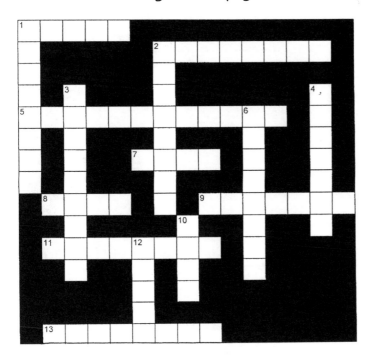

The first Pilgrim baby born in the New World was a boy named Peregrine. His name means "wanderer". He lived to be eighty-three years old and died only ten miles from where he was born. He didn't wander much!

ACROSS
1. _____ Treaty signed with the Indians
2. Town where the Pilgrims settled
5. Holiday first celebrated here
7. Planted with seeds as fertilizer
8. The first winter the weather was very _____.
9. Indian who first walked into the Plantation
11. Puritans wanted freedom to practice their _____
13. Day of the week we celebrate Thanksgiving

DOWN
1. The Pilgrim's religious group
2. The name we have given the Puritans
3. Ship the Puritans sailed on
4. Plymouth Rock is a granite _____.
6. Month we celebrate Thanksgiving
10. The first winter there was not enough _____.
12. At the 3-day celebration they played _____.

What River Am I ? # 1

I begin in the White Mountains of central New Hampshire and flow south through northeastern Massachusetts until I empty into the Atlantic Ocean in Newburyport, Massachusetts. Back in the 1800s, textile mills were built along my banks. I am 110 miles long.

Use the Code Box below to write the letters above the numbered spaces.

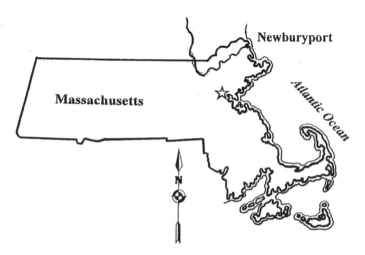

Code Box

S	J	V	D	X	I	Y	P	E	W	K	B	H
1	2	3	4	5	6	7	8	9	10	11	12	13
R	A	Q	N	G	T	L	C	M	U	Z	F	O
14	15	16	17	18	19	20	21	22	23	24	25	26

I flow south through the following Massachusetts towns before reaching the ocean.

20 26 10 9 20 20 ,   20 15 10 14 9 17 21 9 ,

15 17 4   13 15 3 9 14 13 6 20 20

I am the 22 9 14 14 6 22 15 21 11   14 6 3 9 14 .

What River Am I?   #2

I begin in Hopkinton and twist and turn for eighty miles until I empty into Boston Harbor. I separate the cities of Boston and Cambridge and people enjoy jogging, strolling and picnicking along my banks.

Use the Code Box below to write the letters above the numbered spaces.

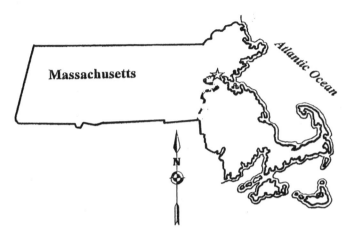

Massachusetts

Atlantic Ocean

N

Code Box

S	J	V	D	X	I	Y	P	E	W	K	B	H
1	2	3	4	5	6	7	8	9	10	11	12	13
R	A	Q	N	G	T	L	C	M	U	Z	F	O
14	15	16	17	18	19	20	21	22	23	24	25	26

Some of the reasons people enjoy me -

$\overline{11}\ \overline{15}\ \overline{7}\ \overline{15}\ \overline{11}\ \overline{6}\ \overline{17}\ \overline{18}$, $\overline{1}\ \overline{15}\ \overline{6}\ \overline{20}\ \overline{6}\ \overline{17}\ \overline{18}$,

$\overline{25}\ \overline{6}\ \overline{1}\ \overline{13}\ \overline{6}\ \overline{17}\ \overline{18}$ and $\overline{21}\ \overline{15}\ \overline{17}\ \overline{26}\ \overline{9}\ \overline{6}\ \overline{17}\ \overline{18}$

I am the $\overline{21}\ \overline{13}\ \overline{15}\ \overline{14}\ \overline{20}\ \overline{9}\ \overline{1}$ $\overline{14}\ \overline{6}\ \overline{3}\ \overline{9}\ \overline{14}$.

What River Am I ? #3

I begin in New Hampshire and cut all the way through central Massachusetts until I empty into Long Island Sound. My name comes from the Algonquian Indian word meaning *on the long tidal river*. I am 407 miles long.

Use the Code Box below to write the letters above the numbered spaces.

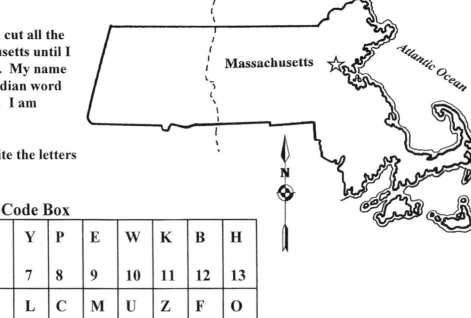

Massachusetts

Atlantic Ocean

N

Code Box

S	J	V	D	X	I	Y	P	E	W	K	B	H
1	2	3	4	5	6	7	8	9	10	11	12	13
R	A	Q	N	G	T	L	C	M	U	Z	F	O
14	15	16	17	18	19	20	21	22	23	24	25	26

48

Along the way I pass through the following cities and towns.

$\overline{17}\ \overline{26}\ \overline{14}\ \overline{19}\ \overline{13}\ \overline{15}\ \overline{22}\ \overline{8}\ \overline{19}\ \overline{26}\ \overline{17}$ ' $\overline{13}\ \overline{26}\ \overline{20}\ \overline{7}\ \overline{26}\ \overline{11}\ \overline{9}$

$\overline{21}\ \overline{13}\ \overline{6}\ \overline{21}\ \overline{26}\ \overline{8}\ \overline{9}\ \overline{9}$ and $\overline{1}\ \overline{8}\ \overline{14}\ \overline{6}\ \overline{17}\ \overline{18}\ \overline{25}\ \overline{6}\ \overline{9}\ \overline{20}\ \overline{4}$

I am the $\overline{21}\ \overline{26}\ \overline{17}\ \overline{17}\ \overline{9}\ \overline{21}\ \overline{19}\ \overline{6}\ \overline{21}\ \overline{23}\ \overline{19}$ $\overline{14}\ \overline{6}\ \overline{3}\ \overline{9}\ \overline{14}$.

CRANBERRY MAZE

Massachusetts grows more cranberries than any other state. We call the place where cranberries grow a BOG. Help the grower find his way to the cranberry vine in the maze.

↰ Start here

49

SKIER'S WORD SEARCH

Whether you Alpine or Nordic ski, snowboard or snowshoe you can pick and choose among Massachusetts' exciting slopes. Find and circle 14 popular ski resorts in the word search. They may be spelled forward, backward, upside down, or diagonally. The space between words (i.e. Mt. Tom) has been eliminated in the puzzle.

Y	D	R	O	F	N	A	L	B	K	M	B	B
B	E	B	R	O	D	I	E	A	T	K	U	E
R	B	L	F	O	J	Z	E	T	O	C	T	R
A	S	Q	L	Y	B	P	O	O	H	U	T	K
D	H	I	M	A	Y	M	O	D	C	R	E	S
F	R	P	H	N	V	V	G	N	I	B	R	H
O	O	L	I	H	T	A	H	Z	R	S	N	I
R	M	M	V	Y	G	K	B	G	E	N	U	R
D	I	C	O	V	B	D	A	O	J	N	T	E
J	B	O	U	S	Q	U	E	T	H	I	U	B
I	T	N	U	O	M	A	T	A	C	S	J	C
X	P	S	L	L	I	H	E	U	L	B	A	B
N	O	R	T	H	F	I	E	L	D	I	L	N

BERKSHIRE
BLANFORD
BLUE HILLS
BOUSQUET
BRADFORD

BRODIE
BUTTERNUT
CATAMOUNT
INNSBRUCK
JERICHO

JIMINY PEAK
MT. TOM
NASHOBA VALLEY
NORTHFIELD

The Freedom Trail

In the 1950s the people of Boston realized how difficult it was for visitors to see all of Boston's great historical sites. So they created The Freedom Trail, a red painted stripe that guides people along a 2.5-mile route that celebrates the city's role in our country's early struggle for freedom.

Place a check in the box next to each of the 16 sites that you have visited.

❑ 1. The Trail begins at the *Boston Common*, America's oldest public park. Try skating on the Frog Pond in the winter!

❑ 2. The gold domed *State House* is where the state government meets and conducts its business.

❑ 3. *Park Street Church* used to be called "Brimstone Corner" because gunpowder was stored here during the War of 1812.

❑ 4. *The Granary Burial Ground* holds the graves of such famous Americans as John Hancock, Paul Revere, Sam Adams and the victims of the Boston Massacre. Can you find the grave of Elizabeth Vergoose ~ better known as Mother Goose?

❑ 5. *King's Chapel* was founded in 1688. Prisoners came here for a last sermon before being hanged on Boston Common.

❑ 6. *Ben Franklin's Statue and the site of the first public school.* Built in 1635, Samuel Adams, Benjamin Franklin and Cotton Mather were all students at the first public school in America.

❑ 7. *The Old Corner Bookstore* was built in 1712 and was an important gathering spot for such great American authors as Longfellow, Emerson, Hawthorne and Thoreau.

8. *The Old South Meeting House* is where Patriots, dressed as Mohawk Indians, met for the beginning of the Boston Tea Party. Today you can see a multimedia exhibition that brings American history to life.

9. *The Old State House* was built in 1713. On July 18, 1776 the Declaration of Independence was read in public for the first time from the balcony here.

10. *Boston Massacre Site.* A circle of cobblestones marks where the first blood of the American Revolution was shed on March 5, 1770. Crispus Attucks, the first African-American patriot, was killed that day.

11. *Faneuil Hall* was built in 1742 to be used for public meetings and as a marketplace. The Hall is known as the *Cradle of Liberty* because of all the speeches given here calling for independence and freedom.

12. *Paul Revere's House* was built in 1680 and is the oldest surviving structure in Boston.

13. *Old North Church.* On April 18, 1775 two lanterns were hung from the church steeple warning the colonists that the British were coming to attack them by water. Do you know the poem that reads, *One if by land, two if by sea.......?*

14. *Copp's Hill Burial Ground* began when Kings Chapel cemetery got over crowded. The British fired their canon from here at the colonists on Bunker Hill.

15. *USS Constitution*, located in Charlestown, is nicknamed "Old Ironsides" because the British cannonballs bounced off her sides.

16. *Bunker Hill Monument* commemorates the first major battle of the Revolution. The colonists were told, *Don't shoot until you see the whites of their eyes!*

52

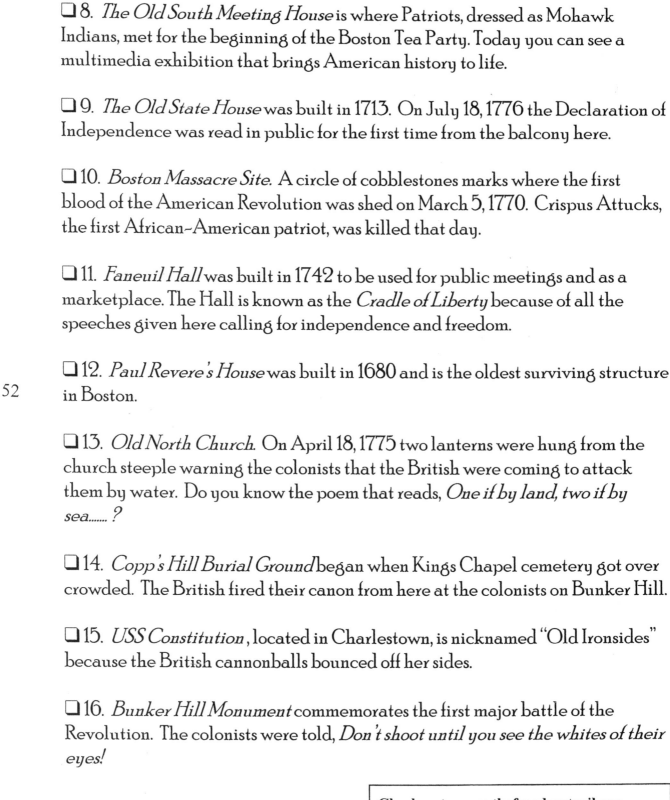

Check out: **www.thefreedomtrail.org**
www.nps.gov

Freedom Trail Criss-Cross

Below are listed just some of the people and things you'll learn about or see when you walk the Freedom Trail. Fit the words into the puzzle squares. The clues are listed alphabetically according to the number of letters in each word.

53

3 Letters	5 Letters	7 Letters	9 Letters	10 Letters
WAR	HILLS	HISTORY	BOOKSTORE	BUNKER HILL
	TRAIL		COLONISTS	
4 Letters		8 Letters	COPPS HILL	11 Letters
MAPS	6 Letters	FROG POND	GRAVEYARD	FANEUIL HALL
SHIP	BOSTON	GOLD DOME	RED STRIPE	
	CHURCH	MONUMENT		12 Letters
	REVERE			COBBLESTONES
	SCHOOL			

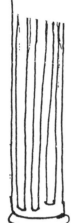

MASSACHUSETTS MUSEUMS

There are many exciting museums in Massachusetts outside of Boston. Find the location of each museum listed below by using the Code Box.

Code Box

S	J	V	D	X	I	Y	P	E	W	K	B	H
1	2	3	4	5	6	7	8	9	10	11	12	13
R	A	Q	N	G	T	L	C	M	U	Z	F	O
14	15	16	17	18	19	20	21	22	23	24	25	26

54

1. The location of The Cape Cod Museum of Natural History (www.ccmnh.org)

  $\frac{}{12}$ $\frac{}{14}$ $\frac{}{9}$ $\frac{}{10}$ $\frac{}{1}$ $\frac{}{19}$ $\frac{}{9}$ $\frac{}{14}$

2. The location of the Essex Peabody Museum (www.pem.org)

  $\frac{}{1}$ $\frac{}{15}$ $\frac{}{20}$ $\frac{}{9}$ $\frac{}{22}$

3. The location of the DeCordova Museum and Sculpture Park
(www.decordova.org)

  $\frac{}{20}$ $\frac{}{6}$ $\frac{}{17}$ $\frac{}{21}$ $\frac{}{26}$ $\frac{}{20}$ $\frac{}{17}$

4. The location of Harvard Museums of Natural History
(www.hmnh.harvard.edu)

  $\frac{}{21}$ $\frac{}{15}$ $\frac{}{22}$ $\frac{}{12}$ $\frac{}{14}$ $\frac{}{6}$ $\frac{}{4}$ $\frac{}{18}$ $\frac{}{9}$

Cross-Outs #2

Follow the instructions to find an interesting fact about Massachusetts.

1. Cross out 4 colors.
2. Cross out 3 animals.
3. Cross out 4 numbers.
4. Cross out 4 sports.

BLUE	BOSTON	SEVEN	YELLOW	CAT
IS	TEN	BLACK	THE	SIX
COW	STATE	HORSE	SOCCER	FOOTBALL
CAPITAL	FORTY	TENNIS	ORANGE	BASEBALL

Follow the instructions to find another interesting fact about Massachusetts.

1. Cross out 3 birds.
2. Cross out 4 boys names.
3. Cross out 3 types of transportation.
4. Cross out 2 pieces of furniture.

OWL	HARVARD	BLUE JAY	WAS	JACK
THE	RANDY	CAR	FIRST	WILLIAM
BICYCLE	COLLEGE	GULL	TRAIN	IN
THE	TOM	CHAIR	COUNTRY	BED

The Dot Game

This game needs two players. Take turns drawing a horizontal or vertical line between two dots. The player that draws a line that completes a square writes his or her initial inside that completed square. It helps if you each use a different colored pencil or pen. When all the squares are connected, count how many squares each player finished. Squares are worth one point each or two points if it contains a basketball. Whoever has the most points wins.

56

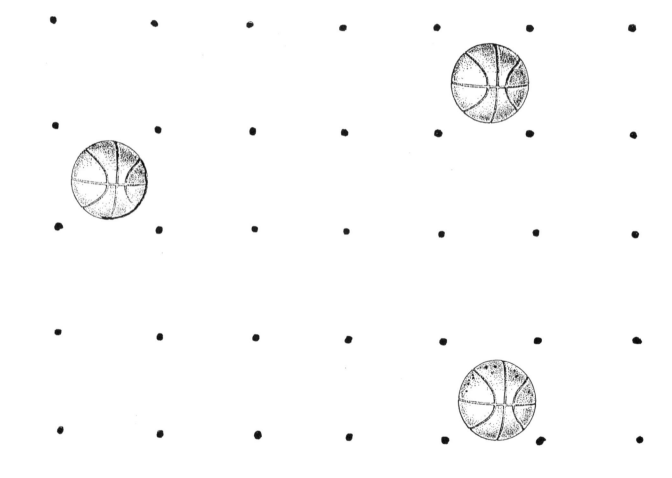

Have you visited the Basketball Hall of Fame in Springfield?
Check it out on the web at www.hoophall.com

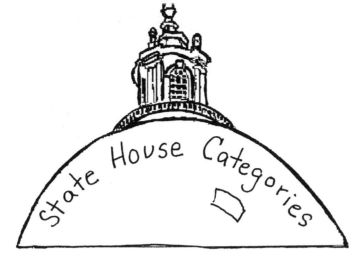

The shiny gold dome of the Massachusetts State House marks the spot where the state government conducts its business. It sits high up on Beacon Hill in the capital city of Boston. Under each category below list one thing that begins with every letter. For example under the category **FOOD**, you might list beans or butter or bread next to the letter B.

FOOD

B _____

O _____

S _____

T _____

O _____

N _____

BIRDS OR ANIMALS

B _____

O _____

S _____

T _____

O _____

N _____

KIDS' NAMES

B _____

O _____

S _____

T _____

O _____

N _____

TOWNS IN MASSACHUSETTS

B _____

O _____

S _____

T _____

O _____

N _____

More Massachusetts Museums

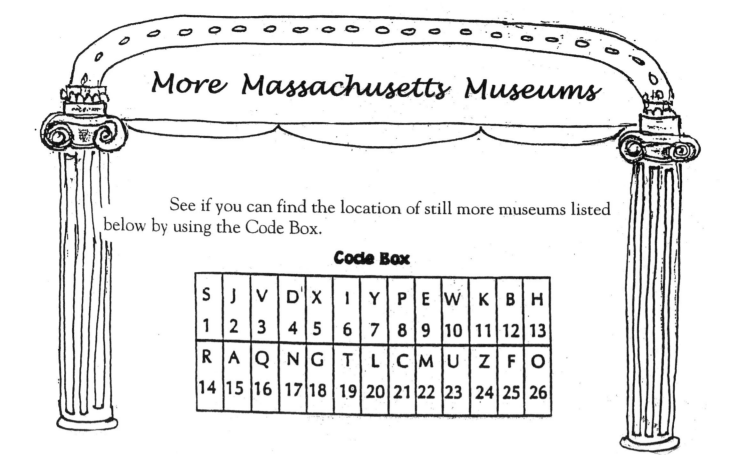

See if you can find the location of still more museums listed below by using the Code Box.

Code Box

S	J	V	D	X	I	Y	P	E	W	K	B	H
1	2	3	4	5	6	7	8	9	10	11	12	13
R	A	Q	N	G	T	L	C	M	U	Z	F	O
14	15	16	17	18	19	20	21	22	23	24	25	26

58

1. The location of the American Textile History Museum (www.athm.org)

     __ __ __ __ __ __
     20 26 10 9 20 20

2. The location of the Basketball Hall of Fame (www.hoophall.com)

     __ __ __ __ __ __ __ __ __ __ __
     1 8 14 6 17 18 25 6 9 20 4

3. The location of the Cape Cod Children's Museum
(www.capecodchildrensmuseum.pair.com)

     __ __ __ __ __ __ __
     22 15 1 13 8 9 9

4. The location of the EcoTarium (www.ecotarium.org)

     __ __ __ __ __ __ __ __ __
     10 26 14 21 9 1 19 9 14

Hidden Message Word Search # 2

Find the words listed below and circle them in the puzzle. Put a cross through the word after you have circled it.

It's my way or the highway!

King James

```
T F O O L I S H H E
P A I N T I N G S P
U R N L O B S T E R
I F R E I T A N S Y
S T E E R T S F O P
U N D N T D T E D P
B O S T W N L L O A
N A E C O A I I E H
Y T T E R P Y W H N
S R E V I R Y P O C
```

59

CHILDREN
FOOLISH
LOBSTER
PRETTY
WINTER

COPY
HAPPY
OCEAN
RIVERS

FENWAY
LITTLE
PAINTINGS
STREETS

Now fill in the spaces below with the letters that were left uncircled in the Word Search. You will discover an interesting fact about Massachusetts.

___ _____ _____

_____ .

Cape Cod Cross-Outs

Follow the instructions to find an interesting fact about Cape Cod.

1. Cross out 4 pieces of furniture.
2. Cross out 3 farm animals.
3. Cross out 3 trees.
4. Cross out 3 girls names.

CHAIR	CAPE	PIG	OAK	BED
COD	MAPLE	DESK	IS	A
MEGAN	HOOK	GOAT	TABLE	KATE
SHAPED	ROOSTER	PENINSULA	JANE	PINE

60

Follow the instructions to find another interesting fact about Cape Cod.

1. Cross out 3 kinds of weather.
2. Cross out 4 birds.
3. Cross out 4 colors.
4. Cross out 4 boys names.

CHICKADEE	THE	RED	RAIN	PILGRIMS
BROWN	SPARROW	SETTLED	ROBIN	ORANGE
SNOW	SAM	KEVIN	IN	WIND
JOHN	PLYMOUTH	EAGLE	PURPLE	MICHAEL

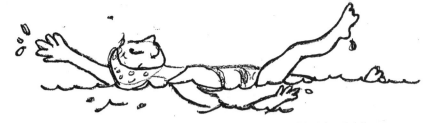

HISTORICAL VS. SEASHORE

Some people love to see Massachusetts many historical sights. Others love to visit our beautiful beaches. The words HISTORICAL and SEASHORE each have many smaller words inside them. For example, from the letters HISTORICAL you can spell CHART and TRAIL. Which do you think has more words in it? Make a list from each word.

SCORING
3-letter word = 1 point
4-letter word = 2 points
5-letter word = 3 points
Add one point for each additional letter.

HISTORICAL

points

_____
_____
_____
_____
_____
_____
_____
_____
_____
_____
_____
_____
_____
_____

SEASHORE

points

_____
_____
_____
_____
_____
_____
_____
_____
_____
_____
_____
_____
_____
_____

THE DOT GAME

This game needs two players. Take turns drawing a horizontal or vertical line between two dots. The player that draws a line that completes a square writes his or her initial inside that completed square. It helps if you each use a different colored pencil or pen. When all the squares are connected, count how many squares each player completed. Each completed square is worth one point or two points if it contains a snowflake.

Your scores: Player 1 _____   Player 2 _____

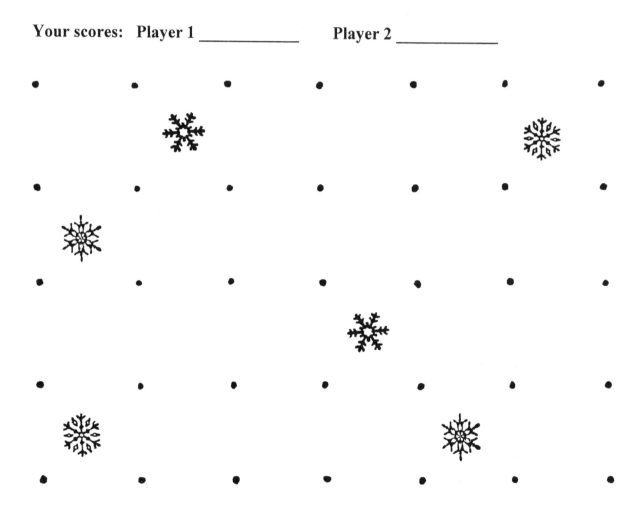

62

Did you know that while no two snowflakes are exactly the same all snowflakes have six sides?

THE MASSACHUSETTS CRANBERRY HARVEST FESTIVAL

The cranberry is a native American fruit that grows on trailing vines like a strawberry. Because they are rich in Vitamin C sailors used to eat them on long voyages to prevent scurvy.

The Cranberry Harvest Festival is held in Plymouth County usually on Columbus Day Weekend to celebrate the harvest. They offer tours of bogs, cooking demonstrations, crafts, music, children's entertainment and rides.
Check out www.cranberries.org/festival .

Many delicious foods and products are made with cranberries. Find and circle them in the word search puzzle below.

BREAD
BUCKLE
CAKE
CANDY
CRUMBLE
ICE CREAM
JAM
JELLIES
JUICE
MUFFINS
PIES
PUDDING
SALADS
SAUCES
SOAP
TARTS

J	B	I	M	U	F	F	I	N	S	P
O	U	R	C	P	P	A	O	S	I	I
D	Q	I	E	E	P	M	B	E	H	X
S	S	N	C	A	C	K	S	C	Z	S
E	D	V	H	E	D	R	R	K	T	S
I	A	P	J	Y	E	U	E	R	K	E
L	L	C	I	L	M	C	A	A	S	C
L	A	L	K	B	A	T	C	M	M	U
E	S	C	L	N	P	F	A	A	B	A
J	U	E	D	J	A	M	U	U	K	S
B	I	Y	G	N	I	D	D	U	P	E

TIP

Cranberry Recipes

Cranberry Velvet

1 lb. can whole cranberry sauce
1 cup crushed pineapple, drained
2 Tablespoons lemon juice
Dash of salt
1/4 lb. miniature marshmallows
1 cup heavy cream, whipped

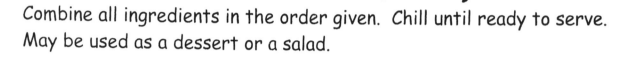

Combine all ingredients in the order given. Chill until ready to serve.
May be used as a dessert or a salad.

64

Yummy Cranberry Pudding

1 ½ Tablespoons butter
1 cup sugar
½ cup milk

1 teaspoon cinnamon
1 cup flour
1 ½ teaspoons baking powder
2 cups raw cranberries

Preheat oven to 375 degrees

Cream the butter and sugar together. Add the milk, flour, cinnamon and baking powder. Add the cranberries. Pour the batter into a buttered and floured dish. Bake for 30 minutes. Serve with vanilla ice cream.
Serves 6.

MA

The U. S. Post Office's two-letter abbreviation for the Commonwealth of Massachusetts is MA - the first two letters of its name. The answer to each definition below is a word containing the letters MA.

1. It covers your face on Halloween   <u>M</u>   <u>A</u> __ __

2. Messages you get on the computer   __ <u>M</u> <u>A</u> __ __

3. A grown-up girl   __ __ <u>M</u> <u>A</u> __

4. A punctuation mark   __ __ __ <u>M</u> <u>A</u>

5. He delivers the mail   __ __ __ __ <u>M</u> <u>A</u> __

6. A man with more than human powers   __ __ __ __ __ <u>M</u> <u>A</u> __   65

VISIT MASSACHUSETTS IN THE SUMMER

You are in charge of trying to get tourists to come and visit Massachusetts. In the frame below, make your own poster or brochure that would encourage people to come to Massachusetts in the SUMMER.

66

VISIT MASSACHUSETTS IN THE WINTER

You are in charge of trying to get tourists to come and visit Massachusetts. In the frame below, make your own poster or brochure that would encourage people to come to Massachusetts in the WINTER.

67

A CLAM EATING CONTEST

A group of children held a clam eating contest. Read all the clues. Then write the correct names next to the number of clams he or she ate.

NAME	NUMBER OF CLAMS
A. _____	16
B. _____	12
C. _____	10
D. _____	6
E. _____	4

68

1. Taylor ate the most clams.

2. Gabe ate 10 less than Taylor

3. Holly did not eat more than Gabe.

4. Sam ate more than Gabe, but less than Emily.

The town of Ipswich is famous for their clams that live in the tidal flats.

Q: Why won't a clam lend you money?
A: Because they are shellfish.

MAPPING MASSACHUSETTS

Map makers place horizontal and vertical lines on maps to make it easier to find places on a map. The lines of the grid divide the map into imaginary squares. Look across the top of the map below for the numbers. Then look down the left edge of the map for the letters. The letter-number combination is called a *coordinate.*

Use the grid map below to find the location of each of the places listed below. Example: Boston, the capital of Massachusetts, is located within which coordinates? Answer: B4

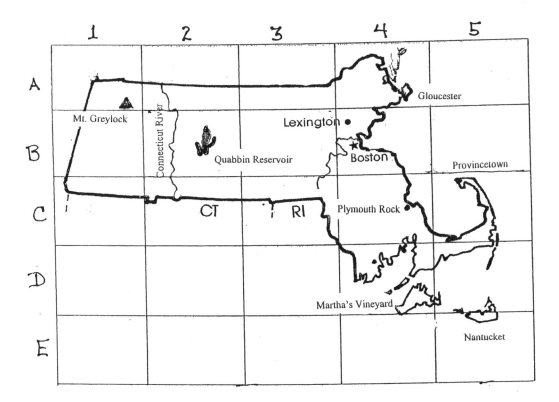

69

Coordinate

_____ Gloucester

_____ Provincetown

_____ Nantucket Island

_____ Martha's Vineyard

Coordinate

__B 4__ Boston

_____ The Quabbin Reservoir

_____ Mt. Greylock

_____ Lexington

Your Massachusetts Alphabet

Authors and illustrators are always making new alphabet books about places and things that interest them. If you were to write and illustrate your own personal Alphabet of Massachusetts you might start with "A is for Algonquian" or "B is for the Berkshires". In the following boxes design and than draw a picture for your own personal Massachusetts Alphabet.

70

A is for _____

B is for _____

C is for _____

D is for _____

Your Massachusetts Alphabet

E is for _____

F is for _____

G is for _____

H is for _____

Your Massachusetts Alphabet

I is for _____

J is for _____

72

K is for _____

L is for _____

Your Massachusetts Alphabet

M^{is for}_____

N^{is for}_____

O^{is for}_____

P^{is for}_____

Your Massachusetts Alphabet

Q is for _____

R is for _____

S is for _____

T is for _____

Your Massachusetts Alphabet

U is for _____

V is for _____

W is for _____

X is for _____

75

Your Massachusetts Alphabet

Here are some suggestions:

A is for Appleseed, Algonquian, Adams, Athenaeum

B is for Beacon Hill, the Big Dig, Boston, Baked Beans, Bunker Hill

C is for Castle Island, Chinatown, the Common

D is for Durgin-Park, Mary Dyer

E is for Emerald Necklace

F is for Faneuil Hall, Freedom Trail, Frog Pond, Fenway Park

G is for Gristmill

H is for Harvard, Hatch Shell, Holocaust Memorial, "The Hub"

I is for Irish, Ironsides, Islands, Immigrants

J is for Jamaica Pond

K is for King Philip's War, Kennedy

L is for Louisburg Square, Longfellow

M is for Museums, Molasses Explosion, Marathon, Minutemen

N is for North End, Nantucket

O is for Old North Church

P is for The Pops, Public Garden, Puritans, Pilgrams

Q is for Quincy Market, Quahogs, Quabbin Reservoir

R is for Paul Revere, Roxbury, Redcoats, Red Sox

S is for "Southie", State House, Symphony Hall, Swan Boats

T is for the "T", Triple Deckers

U is for Union Oyster House

V is for the Vikings, Visitors

W is for Whelks, Whales

X is for xmas

Y is for Ye Olde Union Oyster House

Z is for Zoo

Sightseeing Around Boston

Take the "T" (the subway), walk the Freedom Trail (a red painted line),
ride a Duck bus or tour on a trolley but be sure to visit Boston's fun spots.
Find and circle these popular attractions in the word search.

AQUARIUM
BUNKER HILL
CHILDREN'S MUSEUM
CHINATOWN
FANEUIL HALL
FENWAY PARK

KENNEDY LIBRARY
MUSEUM OF SCIENCE
OLD STATE HOUSE
PUBLIC GARDEN
QUINCY MARKET
TEA PARTY SHIP

```
M  K  E  N  N  E  D  Y  L  I  B  R  A  R  Y
U  U  N  E  D  R  A  G  C  I  L  B  U  P  C
E  P  S  B  U  N  K  E  R  H  I  L  L  H  F
S  I  W  E  H  U  U  G  C  C  O  Y  I  B  A
U  H  N  K  U  T  B  N  J  R  D  D  K  U  N
O  S  W  Y  J  M  Y  T  L  Y  R  F  V  M  E
H  Y  O  E  M  N  O  R  F  E  E  R  T  U  U
E  T  T  R  M  M  Y  F  N  F  Z  U  B  I  I
T  R  A  R  N  S  A  S  S  W  A  O  V  R  L
A  A  N  I  H  V  M  M  D  C  Q  T  S  A  H
T  P  I  K  N  U  G  U  W  I  I  B  U  U  A
S  A  H  O  S  U  H  S  P  C  K  E  P  Q  L
D  E  C  E  E  K  O  Z  I  F  F  N  A  L
L  T  U  F  E  N  W  A  Y  P  A  R  K  C  W
O  M  T  E  K  R  A  M  Y  C  N  I  U  Q  E
```

ACROSTICS

An acrostic is a verse that is written using the first letters of a word or phrase. It may or may not rhyme. Here is an acrostic of the word *whale*.

Wondrous beasts
Hurtling through the sea
All shimmery and sleek
Looking for feasts
Endlessly.

Below is another example of an acrostic using the word *ocean*.

Over the waves a boat sails
Carrying children with shovels and pails
Eager to land on a sandy shore
And build tall castles and dragons that roar
Now they can let their imaginations soar!

And here is an acrostic created from the word *sea*.

Salty
Emerald colored
Always changing.

Create Your Own Acrostic

Make up and illustrate your own acrostic on this page using the words provided.

G_____

U_____

L_____

L_____

B_____

O_____

S_____

T_____

O_____

N_____

C_____

O_____

D_____

Historic Deerfield

Historic Deerfield is a museum of New England history and art within the 328 year old village of Deerfield. Thousands of people come here every year to explore what American life was like between 1650 and 1850. Here are some things you can do as you walk all around the village.

- Go to Memorial Hall Museum to see the door that still has the hole made by Indian tomahawks in the famous 1704 raid.
- Cook over an open hearth and play 18th-century games.
- Visit the gift shop for a copy of *The Boy Captive of Old Deerfield* by Mary P. Wells Smith.
- In April help with the sheep shearing. Gather the raw wool fleece and practice carding, spinning and weaving yarn into cloth.
- Learn about sweetgrass and how the fragrant fibers were woven into baskets.
- Explore the beautiful trails and fields of Deerfield.
- Visit at Halloween and take a hayride. Go on a tour of the Old Burying Ground.
- Hear about the importance of tea in 18th century New England and meet a Redcoat.
- Drive or hike up Mount Sugarloaf to feast on the beauty of the Pioneer Valley.
- Play the hurdy gurdy ~ a musical toy operated by a hand crank.

Get ready for your trip by visiting online at:
www.historic-deerfield.org

Crossword Puzzle #2
"Historic Deerfield"

After reading about things to do in Historic Deerfield, try your hand at this crossword puzzle.

ACROSS

4. Deerfield is located in a old New England _____.
5. Thousands of _____ come each year.
7. Raw wool _____ comes from sheep.
8. Located in the _____ Valley.
10. An important hot drink
11. Woven from sweetgrass
13. Look down on the Valley from Mount _____ .
14. _____ over open hearths.
15. Historic Deerfield is a _____.

DOWN

1. Hike or _____ up Mount Sugarloaf
2. What villagers cooked over
3. In April, come help shear ____ .
6. Fragrant fibers used in baskets
9. Play 18th century _____.
10. A hurdy gurdy is a musical _____.
12. You can ____ all around the village.

WHEN I VISITED MASSACHUSETTS

THE NEXT TIME I AM IN MASSACHUSETTS I WANT TO

_____

_____

_____

_____

THE THING I LIKE MOST ABOUT MASSACHUSETTS IS

_____

_____

SOMETHING I LEARNED IN MASSACHUSETTS THAT I DIDN'T KNOW ABOUT BEFORE

_____

_____

_____

WHEN I VISITED MASSACHUSETTS

THINGS I HAD NEVER TASTED BEFORE

_____

_____

_____

_____

SOMETHING I HAD NEVER HEARD BEFORE

_____

_____

MY FAVORITE THING TO DO IN MASSACHUSETTS

_____

_____

_____

THE DOT GAME

This game needs two players. Take turns drawing a horizontal or vertical line between two dots. The player that draws a line that completes a square writes his or her initial inside that completed square. It helps if you each use a different colored pencil or pen. When all the squares are connected, count how many squares each player finished. Squares are worth one point each or two points if it contains a swan. Whoever has the most points wins!

84

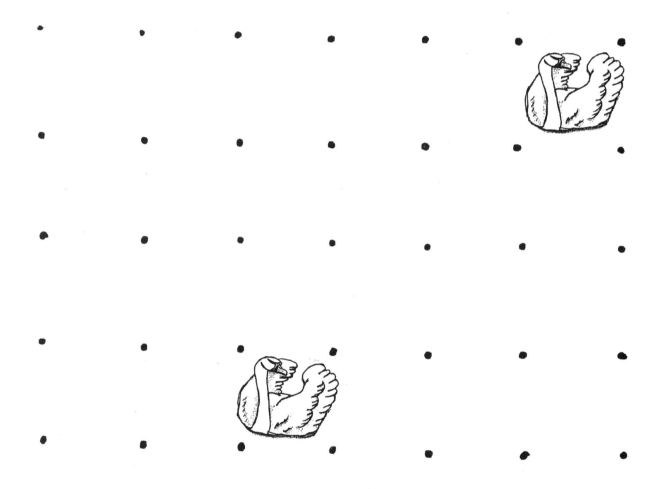

The swan boats in Boston's Public Garden are a popular attraction!

ALL THE ANSWERS

PAGE 6 The Salem Witch Museum

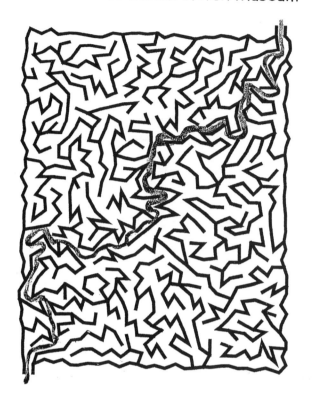

PAGE 9 Arnold Arboretum Maze

PAGE 7   Sea Glass

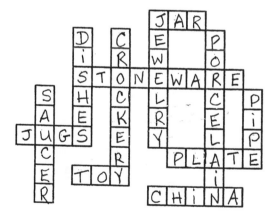

PAGE 10   Criss Cross Capes

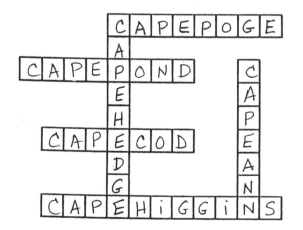

PAGE 11   The Old Ball Game

1. _B_ Baseball
2. _E_ Football
3. _A_ Basketball
4. _D_ Hockey
5. _C_ Soccer

1. _B_ Red Sox
2. _A_ Patriots
3. _C_ Celtics
4. _C_ Bruins
5. _A_ Revolution

PAGE 12   Searching for Seuss

SEAT	_S_	TEA	
SPRING	_P_	RINGS	
TIRE	_R_	TIE	
HIDES	_i_	SHED	
WINTER	_N_	WRITE	
GHOST	_G_	SHOT	
FEAT	_E_	ATE	
IRATE	_i_	TEAR	
BEAST	_E_	STAB	
LEAST	_L_	SEAT	
DREAM	_D_	MARE	

86

PAGE 14   True or False

TRUE	FALSE	BLANK
(L)	B	_L_
F	(A)	_A_
E	(D)	_D_
(Y)	S	_Y_
T	(B)	_B_
(U)	K	_U_
(G)	L	_G_

PAGE 15   Good Neighbors

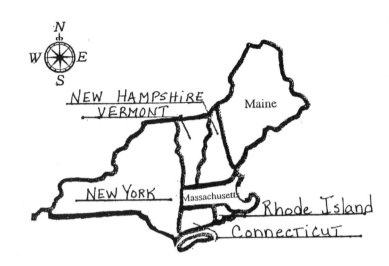

NEW HAMPSHIRE
VERMONT
Maine
NEW YORK
Massachusetts
Rhode Island
Connecticut

PAGE 17   Famous from Massachusetts

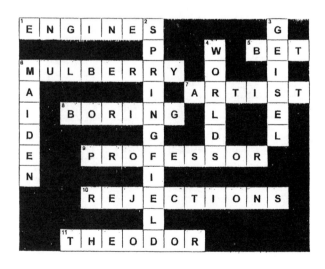

ALL THE ANSWERS

PAGE 18 Mitten Match

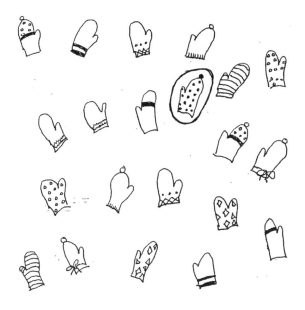

PAGE 20 How Many Miles?

1. The Johnston family first drove from their home in Boston to the city of Lowell to learn about the Industrial Revolution at the Tsongas Industrial History Center. They drove __30__ miles.

2. From Lowell they traveled west to historic Deerfield to visit this living museum. They drove __80__ miles.

3. From Deerfield the family headed to Cheshire where they climbed Mt. Greylock, the highest point in Massachusetts. They drove __46__ miles.

4. From Cheshire they headed east to Concord to visit the Old North Bridge. They wanted to see for themselves where "the shot heard round the world" was fired and the American Revolution began. They drove __146__ miles.

5. Leaving Concord the family headed south to New Bedford overlooking Buzzards Bay. They spent the day visiting the Whaling Museum. They drove __72__ miles.

6. The Johnstons left New Bedford and drove northeast to Plymouth to view Plymouth Rock where the Pilgrims first set foot on the new land. They drove __32__ miles.

7. Finally, our weary travelers drove from Plymouth back home to Boston. They drove __41__ miles.

Question: How many miles did the Johnston family travel that summer?
Answer: __447__ miles

PAGE 19 Boston Harbor Criss Cross

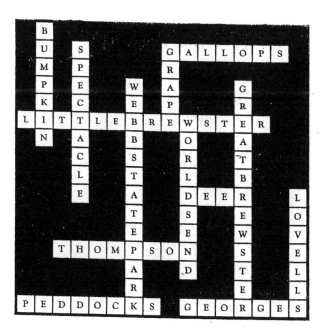

PAGE 22 Mummy in a Maze

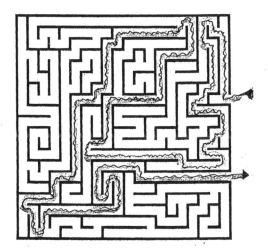

PAGE 23 Search for History

SELDOM __L__ DOMES
HOIST __O__ THIS
WOUND __W__ UNDO
PRIEST __E__ STRIP
LEAST __L__ SEAT
SELDOM __L__ MODES

PAGE 25 Quabbin Word Search

L	E	T	M	W	M	U	S	S	O	P	P	O
P	E	N	A	E	X	Y	K	R	E	T	T	O
X	M	M	I	C	B	A	T	I	P	A	M	K
J	I	F	M	P	B	V	G	Z	S	F	C	D
S	N	O	E	I	U	O	E	L	H	U	F	U
T	K	X	C	D	N	C	B	R	H	Q	O	C
I	S	K	J	A	F	G	R	C	M	O	I	S
B	S	H	Y	I	E	R	D	O	U	I	N	I
B	Z	V	S	T	E	O	Q	M	P	Q	N	L
A	B	H	O	V	O	T	B	H	O	R	P	E
R	E	Y	A	W	Z	K	J	P	J	O	Y	Y
R	O	E	B	E	A	R	T	W	Y	H	S	M
C	B	M	U	S	K	R	A	T	G	X	Z	E

PAGE 28 Old Granary Maze

88

PAGE 27   Following Directons

NORTHWEST   NORTHEAST
SOUTHWEST   SOUTHEAST

1. The Quabbin Reservoir is NORTHWEST of Worcester.

2. Pittsfield is NORTHWEST of Springfield.

3. Springfield is SOUTHWEST of the Quabbin Reservoir.

4. Salem NORTHEAST of Boston.

5. Plymouth Rock is SOUTHEAST of Boston.

6. Nantucket Island is SOUTHEAST of The New Bedford Whaling Museum.

7. Buzzards Bay is SOUTHWEST of Cape Cod Bay.

8. The Cape Cod National Seashore is SOUTHEAST of Boston.

9. The Merrimack River is Northwest of Gloucester.

10. Lowell is Northwest of Boston.

11. Ipswich Bay is Northeast of Boston.

PAGE 29   Secret Messages

1. THE ALGONQUIAN INDIANS

2. FREEDOM OF RELIGION

3. THE EMERALD NECKLACE

4. BLACK HERITAGE TRAIL

PAGE 30 Hidden Message
Word Search #1

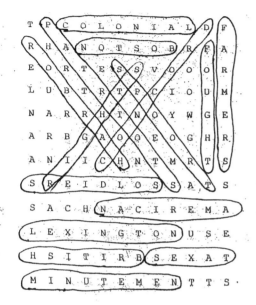

THE REVOLUTIONARY WAR
BEGAN IN MASSACHUSETTS.

PAGE 31 Missing Letters

MEANT _N_ TEAM
NOOSE _E_ SOON
WILT _W_ LIT

STEAM _E_ MAST
PANT _N_ TAP
GROUP _G_ POUR
STEAL _L_ SEAT
STARING _A_ STRING
GRAND _N_ DRAG
DREAD _D_ READ

STARE _A_ REST
QUEST _Q_ SUET
SUNDAY _U_ SANDY
STATE _A_ TEST
STRIDE _R_ DIETS
CASHIER _I_ SEARCH
UNDER _U_ NERD
MINTY _M_ TINY

PAGE 34 Algonquian Words
Game

Here are some of our words:

alert, anger, beast, blasting, blog, boring, brain, bring, equations, giant, gloating, globe, grain, great, guest, quaint, quart, questioning, quiet, quotes, slant, stain, string, strong, suntan, sorting, trails, train, triangles

PAGE 35 Cross-Outs #1

MOUNT	LION	GREYLOCK	YELLOW	FLY
TIGER	IS	ZEBRA	THE	JOHN
HIGHEST	GREEN	ANT	PINK	POINT
BEE	IN	GIRAFFE	THE	STATE

**Mount Greylock is the
highest point in the state.**

89

MATH	THE	STATE'S	PANTS	NICKNAME
HISTORY	IS	PANDA	THE	PETUNIA
SHIRT	SALMON	APPLE	ENGLISH	DAFFODIL
LEMON	BAY	HAT	STATE	DAISY

**The state's nickname is
The Bay State.**

PAGE #36 Missing Letters

They are the _Taconic_ Mountains.

ALL THE ANSWERS

PAGE 37   The Boston Molasses
Flood Maze

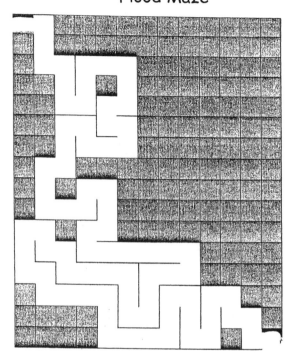

PAGE 41   Seafood Favorites

CHILD	Cod	Quahogs	Clams	Oyster
Bill	X	X	X	O
Sarah	O	X	X	X
Bob	X	X	O	X
Sue	X	O	X	X

PAGE 42   Cape Cod Word Search

90

PAGE 38 Famous from Massachusetts

PAGE 44   The Pilgrims

1. Indian tribe that lived in Massachusetts

W A M P A N O A G
10 15 22 8 15 17 26 15 18

2. The name of the Indian who first helped the Pilgrims

S A M O S E T
1 15 22 26 1 9 19

3. Name of the ship the Puritans sailed on from England.

M A Y F L O W E R
22 15 7 25 20 26 10 9 14

V I S I T   P L I M O T H
3 6 1 6 19   8 20 6 22 26 19 13
P L A N T A T I O N   A N D
8 20 15 17 19 15 19 6 26 17   15 17 4
S E E   H O W   T H E
1 9 9   13 26 10   19 13 9
P I L G R I M S   L I V E D.
8 6 20 18 14 6 22 1   20 6 3 9 4

PAGE 45   Crossword Puzzle #1
"The Pilgrims"

PAGE 46 What River Am I ? #1

I begin in Franklin, New Hampshire and flow south through the following Massachusetts towns before reaching the ocean.

L O W E L L ,   L A W R E N C E ,
20 26 10 9 20 20   20 15 10 14 9 17 21 9
A N D   H A V E R H I L L
15 17 4   13 15 3 9 14 13 6 20 20

I am the   M E R R I M A C K   R I V E R.
22 9 14 14 6 22 15 21 11   14 6 3 9 14

PAGE 47 What River Am I? #2

Some of the reasons people enjoy me -

K A Y A K I N G,   S A I L I N G,
11 15 7 15 11 6 17 18   1 15 6 20 6 17 18

F I S H I N G   and   C A N O E I N G
25 6 1 13 6 17 18   21 15 17 26 9 6 17 18

I am the   C H A R L E S   R I V E R
21 13 15 14 20 9 1   14 6 3 9 14

91

PAGE 48 What River Am I? #3

Along the way I pass through the following cities and towns.

N O R T H A M P T O N,   H O L Y O K E
17 26 14 19 13 15 22 8 19 26 17   13 26 20 7 26 11 9

C H I C O P E E   and   S P R I N G F I E L D
21 13 6 21 26 8 9 9   1 8 14 6 17 18 25 6 9 20 4

I am the C O N N E C T I C U T   R I V E R.
21 26 17 17 9 21 19 6 21 23 19   14 6 3 9 14

PAGE 49 Cranberry Maze

↑ Start here

92

PAGE 53 Freedom Trail Criss Cross

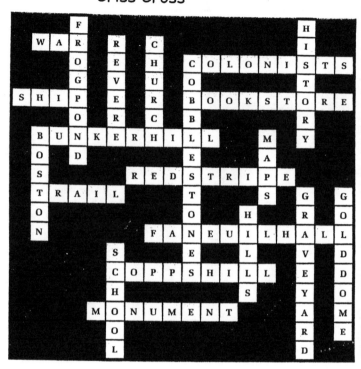

PAGE 50 Skier's Word Search

PAGE 54 Massachusetts Museums

1. The location of The Cape Cod Museum of Natural History (www.ccmnh.org)

B R E W S T E R
12 14 9 10 1 19 9 14

2. The location of the Essex Peabody Museum (www.pem.org)

S A L E M
1 15 20 9 22

3. The location of the DeCordova Museum and Sculpture Park (www.decordova.org)

L I N C O L N
20 6 17 21 26 20 17

4. The location of Harvard Museums of Natural History (www.hmnh.harvard.edu)

C A M B R I D G E
21 15 22 12 14 6 4 18 9

ALL THE ANSWERS

PAGE 55 Cross Outs #2

BLUE	BOSTON	SEVEN	YELLOW	CAT
IS	TEN	BLACK	THE	SIX
COW	STATE	HORSE	SOCCER	FOOTBALL
CAPITAL	FORTY	TENNIS	ORANGE	BASEBALL

BOSTON IS THE STATE CAPITAL.

OWL	HARVARD	BLUE JAY	WAS	JACK
THE	RANDY	CAR	FIRST	WILLIAM
BICYCLE	COLLEGE	GULL	TRAIN	IN
THE	TOM	CHAIR	COUNTRY	BED

HARVARD WAS THE FIRST COLLEGE
IN THE COUNTRY.

PAGE 57 State House Categories

Here are some ideas:
FOOD: bread, butter, broccoli
oysters, oregano, oranges, salt,
sugar, squash, tomato, toast, trout,
onions, okra, olives, nectarines, nuts
KIDS' NAMES: Bob, Beth, Bill, Oliver,
Sam, Shannon, Tom, Tim, Olivia, Oprah,
Nick, Natalie
BIRDS or ANIMALS: bluebirds, orioles,
osprey, sparrow, tortoise, owl, otter,
nightingale, nighthawk
TOWNS IN MASS.: Beverly, Boxford,
Osterville, Somerville, Taunton, Orange,

PAGE 58 More Massachusetts Museums

1. The location of the American Textile History Museum (www.athm.org):

L O W E L L
20 26 10 9 20 20

2. The location of the Basketball Hall of Fame (www.hoophall.com):

S P R I N G F I E L D
1 8 14 6 17 18 25 6 9 20 4

3. The location of the Cape Cod Children's Museum
(www.capecodchildrensmuseum.pair.com):

M A S H P E E
22 15 1 13 8 9 9

4. The location of the EcoTarium (www.ecotarium.org):

W O R C E S T E R
10 26 14 21 9 1 19 9 14

93

Page 59 Hidden Message Word Search #2

THE PURITANS FOUNDED BOSTON

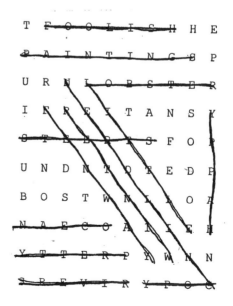

PAGE 60 Cape Cod Cross Outs

CHAIR	CAPE	PIG	OAK	BED
COD	MAPLE	DESK	IS	A
MEGAN	HOOK	GOAT	TABLE	KATE
SHAPED	ROOSTER	PENINSULA	JANE	PINE

CAPE COD IS A HOOK- SHAPED PENINSULA.

CHICKADEE	THE	RED	RAIN	PILGRIMS
BROWN	SPARROW	SETTLED	ROBIN	ORANGE
SNOW	SAM	KEVIN	IN	WIND
JOHN	PLYMOUTH	EAGLE	PURPLE	MICHAEL

THE PILGRIMS SETTLED IN PLYMOUTH.

94

PAGE 61 Historical vs. Seashore

Here are some words we found:
HISTORICAL: chart, trail, slat, this, stir, hoist, oral, coral, rails, cart, art, torch, sort, trash, hit, cast, stoic, short
SEASHORE: she, has, horses, ore, sores, ashes, hoses, eases, rash, hearse, ear, sear, shear, rose, hear, has

PAGE 63 Massachusetts Cranberry Harvest Festival

PAGE 65   MA

1. MASK
2. EMAIL
3. WOMAN
4. COMMA
5. POSTMAN
6. SUPERMAN

PAGE 68 A Clam Eating Contest

Name	# of Clams
A. Taylor	16
B. Emily	12
C. Sam	10
D. Gabe	6
E. Holly	4

ALL THE ANSWERS

PAGE 69 Mapping Massachusetts

Coordinate		Coordinate	
A 4	Gloucester	B 4	Boston
C 5	Provincetown	B 2	The Quabbin Reservoir
E 5	Nantucket Island	A 1	Mt. Greylock
D 4	Martha's Vineyard	B 4	Lexington

PAGE 81   Crossword Puzzle #2
Historic Deerfield

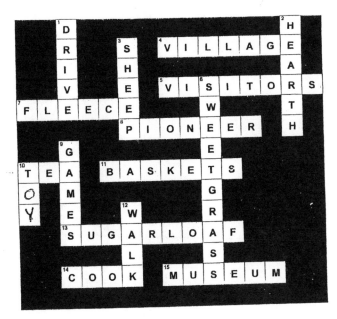

PAGE 77 Sightseeing Around Boston

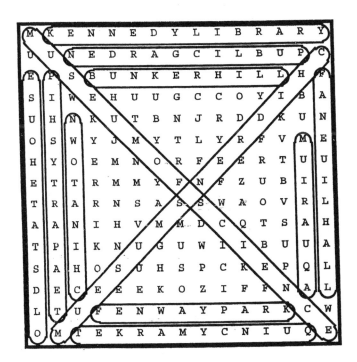